WISDOM
OF THE
WILD

*Life Lessons
from Nature*

WISDOM
OF THE
WILD

SHERI MABRY

CHRONICLE BOOKS
SAN FRANCISCO

Library of Congress Cataloging-in-Publication Data
Names: Mabry, Sheri, author.
Title: Wisdom of the wild : inspiration from nature for living a beautiful life / Sheri Mabry.
Description: San Francisco : Chronicle Books, [2023]
Identifiers: LCCN 2021053516 (print) | LCCN 2021053517 (ebook) | ISBN 9781797208305 (hardback) | ISBN 9781797208312 (ebook)
Subjects: LCSH: Spirituality. | Nature--Religious aspects.
Classification: LCC B105.S64 M33 2022 (print) | LCC B105.S64 (ebook) | DDC 200--dc23/eng/20211117
LC record available at https://lccn.loc.gov/2021053516
LC ebook record available at https://lccn.loc.gov/2021053517

Manufactured in China.

MIX
Paper | Supporting responsible forestry
FSC
www.fsc.org
FSC™ C008047

Design by Rachel Harrell.
Typesetting by Kris Branco.

10 9 8 7 6 5 4 3 2 1

Chronicle books and gifts are available at special quantity discounts to corporations, professional associations, literacy programs, and other organizations. For details and discount information, please contact our premiums department at corporatesales@chroniclebooks.com or at 1-800-759-0190.

Chronicle Books LLC
680 Second Street
San Francisco, California 94107
www.chroniclebooks.com

TO: ALL WHO HELP PRESERVE THE SACRED
PLANET, LEARN FROM IT, AND LOVE FROM IT.

FOR: MY THREE—STAY WILD AND FREE.

~SM

Contents

A Note from the Author

On the first day of an environmental class I took in college, the science professor showed us a tiny box that was sealed shut and asked us to figure out what object from nature was inside without opening it. We used our senses of touch and hearing and smell. And we each wrote down an educated guess based on our past and present experiences. But that wasn't the end of our first assignment. We spent the rest of the semester exploring science, using our experiences in the field to inspire us to adjust our beliefs of what the box held, until the last day of class, when we were given the box again and asked to reevaluate our first answer. What was inside the box? Who had found the correct answer?

In one way, I'll never know, because the professor wouldn't let us open the box to find out. But in another way, I'll always know. Inside the box was mystery. The unopened box inspired us to remain curious and to pursue knowledge, wisdom, and creative thinking. The "rightness" was found in the process. And each of us gained the knowledge that teaching and learning—that life itself, actually—is about the path of exploration. A journey best filled with wonder and a profound sense of awe. It is less about an answer than about the manner in which we experience, which helps us to see things in new ways and allows us to grow, expand, and find peace and balance. That cultivation of curiosity—of seeking the mysteries on a never-ending quest to learn more about our world—can best be experienced through nature, both around us and within. And applying what we learn can help us live the most fulfilling, enriching, gratitude-filled life of potential and possibilities.

I spent countless hours researching the nature facts for this book. But the content on these pages is also a culmination of my humble desire and intention to inspire wonder and an insatiable curiosity in you to learn more about nature. I hope that the words I've written ignite an expanded awe in the mysteries and intricacies of our living planet. I hope this book helps you draw on your own experiences and explore and discover more. And I hope that layered on and around it all will be a new way of looking at and learning about yourself and your full potential.

It is likely that the moment this book is printed, a scientist somewhere will discover that due to one thing, something else has changed, and a scientific detail in this book will become obsolete. It will become "not right." But what I hope will live on long after the book covers are closed is the devotion nurtured in you for the rightness of discovery—a discovery of a life of meaning and unity with nature. And I hope that among other things, this book will in some way serve as that small box that can never be opened . . . a place where wonder is born and sacred mysteries reside. And where the beautiful questions are explored.

With great respect, light, and love,
Sheri

Introduction

The emerald landscape in Ireland, the desert sand dunes in South Africa, the Great Barrier Reef in Australia, Redwood National Park in California—the natural wonders of the world can teach us about mystery, beauty, and awe. Wise people throughout history have always known that nature holds immense power. From religious sources like the Bible and the Buddha to famous thinkers like Albert Einstein, John Muir, Jane Goodall, and Henry David Thoreau, many have found truth and connection in nature. But mystery, beauty, and awe can also be discovered by each of us, within the seemingly commonplace in our natural world, not just in the grandiose. Wonder can be found in the weavings of a tiny bird nest, a chrysalis breaking open, and the slithers of a snake. The everyday occurrences that keep the natural world blooming and buzzing and growing, continually happening to ensure a balanced synthesis of life, can be a source of inspiration, intelligence, and comfort in our lives. Because within the natural world is a natural order—the perpetuation of life itself, unfolding in a delicate rhythm that is present even through destruction, just as a lightning-ignited fire that burns a meadow is the foundation for new growth. Each and every component of nature—from the whale to the housefly—has a critical, divine, and harmonizing part to play in the song of the wild.

So perhaps this complex system of trees and bees and mountains and microorganisms can be more to us than the beauty we've come to embrace and appreciate. If we look deeper, we might be able to discover sacred mystery in these relationships and find inspiration, wisdom, and peace even in the smallest places in the wild. When we continue to observe quietly and peacefully, we'll begin to discover the truth—that after all, we *are* a part of nature and nature is a part of us.

This book is about taking a closer look at the details of our natural world and discovering what we can learn from those details. This collection of life lessons gleaned from the intelligence of nature includes affirmations and self-reflection exercises. It is filled with treasures of wisdom from the wild, how those pieces of nature reflect a lesson on what we can experience in our daily existence, and how we can connect to it and apply it to our daily lives. It draws on research and wisdom from spiritual and humanitarian leaders throughout history who come from different callings. And it celebrates the magic and spirit of our living planet, which can be applied to our daily life to support our deep life work, our purpose, and our soul's calling.

This book can be read in order from beginning to end. Or you might glance through the contents and choose which lesson seems to call to you in the moment. You might use this book as a way to begin or end your day. Or both.

Take this book with you on your own walks in the wild and begin to discover the wisdom that reveals itself to you. Use it as a foundation for discussions with others. Offer it as a gift of gratitude to those you love and even to those you are challenged to love. And please use it to remind yourself of the beautiful connection between your inner self and our living planet.

I hope that when you've finished reading *Wisdom of the Wild*, you'll have a deeper appreciation not only for our living, breathing world, but for your living, breathing self and how they are drawn together to reflect the mysteries of the universe. And I hope you'll go into the wild and *be*, and then share your gratitude for this experience with others.

Live Your Light!
Namaste.

Ants and Beauty

In forests in the Midwest of the United States, ants and trilliums have an interesting partnership. The trillium is so named because of its three leaves and three petals. It is a brilliant, delicate flower that blooms in the spring and spreads across the forest floor in bright spots of mostly pure white. Each delicate beauty can take a long time to flower—up to eight years for a single trillium to blossom. But what's most fascinating about this precious plant is that the seeds drop to the forest floor with a covering that attracts ants. It is so tasty to these little insects that they march the seeds across the forest floor and nibble on the outside as they head toward their nest. When they have eaten what they want, they discard the seeds, giving new trilliums a chance to take root and grow in a place possibly far from where they had fallen to the ground, on a path created by tiny creatures.

CONSIDER

Thinking about the part ants play in the beauty of a spring forest can help us reflect on our own part in helping make the world more beautiful. It might be a stretch to believe that ants are intentionally beautifying a forest; in fact, ants are just being ants. But that doesn't make their contribution any less important. Humans, by nature, create beauty as well, and often we too do it unintentionally—by smiling at others as a habit, picking up discarded trash on our hikes without thinking about it, or creating a home others instinctively want to gather in because it just feels cozy and comforting. Become aware of the ways you express your beauty—both intentionally and unintentionally. This could be expressing yourself through art like painting, sculpture, writing, dance, or composing songs. It could be an expression of beauty through altruistic gestures, empathy, and compassion. It could also be through appreciation or joy. Through clean and resourceful living to minimize the footprint you place on our Earth. Or through peaceful actions. Take note of the ways you beautify the world, give gratitude for doing so, and allow yourself to continue and expand in all the ways you contribute to our planet.

CONNECT

Each evening before sleep, record in a journal all the ways you've beautified the world that day. Review the list and notice that as it grows, you'll become more keenly aware of small acts, thoughts, and sentiments that can make a positive contribution to the planet. There are endless opportunities. Allow the awareness you are developing to then inspire more beautifying. Let it become your practice to recognize and cultivate such beauty steadily.

AFFIRMATION

I commit to expressing, sharing, acting on, and being beautiful through my thoughts, words, and actions, to other humans, to myself, and to our living planet, every day.

Bats and the Intuitive Inner Voice

Bats are fascinating flying mammals. Some help rebuild rainforests by dispersing seeds. Some give birth to their babies upside down and catch them midflight. And many clear the skies of mosquitoes. But one of the most interesting things about bats is that they can make their way through the dark without using their sense of sight. While their day vision works, their nocturnal nature requires that they navigate through the inky skies at night. To stay safe and find what they are looking for, they use echolocation—they rely on their voices, sending out a vibration of sound that bounces off objects, alerting them to where things, prey, and predators are.

CONSIDER

Let's use bats as our models for listening to our own inner voice to find our way—even when things are darkest. Our "echolocation" is our intuition. It is our ability to know the answer that the quiet voice within expresses to us without having to reason. It is that feeling in our gut that acts as a powerful guide. It's the thing that helps us know where we stand in any situation. We are often raised to listen to others' opinions instead of our own: feeling good about ourselves when others approve of us and feeling bad about ourselves when they disapprove of us. Over time, we eventually learn to tune out our own feelings and warning system in favor of outside forces, listening to everyone except ourselves. But what if you turned inward, toward your gut instinct? What if you renewed your ability to listen to that inner voice before you listened to others and honed that skill so that it became your first instinct? Allow your intuition to "bounce off" situations that arise and take the path that you see most clearly, even when things seem dark or challenging to navigate.

CONNECT

▶ Nurture your intuitive voice from within. Close your eyes. Breathe diaphragmatically. To do this, allow your belly to rise on the inhale and fall on the exhale, slowly and steadily, without a pause between the inhale and exhale. Allow your shoulders to remain steady and unmoving. Maintain your focus on this belly breathing for several inhales and exhales.

▶ Next, bring your attention to the situation at hand. Bring awareness to all sensations that arise in both your mind and body, both negative and positive. Imagine and visualize responding to the situation in different ways and continue to adjust your visualized response until the thoughts you are exploring bring a sense of peace and calm instead of angst and stress. When you reach this place of balance, you have aligned your response with your inner intuitive nature.

▶ Practice this listening, looking, and exploring exercise daily, several times a day until the voice of your intuition is loud and clear. Practice honoring the voice of intuition by following its guidance. Then, when facing choices, notice how you can now respond by relying on this inner voice. Adopt the technique of breathing and listening to your own guidance system so that it becomes an ongoing practice.

I check in daily with myself, finding quiet stillness and space to listen to my intuition. When decisions and choices in my life present themselves,

I breathe and quiet the external noise to feel and hear what my inner voice is saying. I trust my inner voice. I trust my intuition. I listen to my intuition.

Bees and Community

Bees buzz all over this planet in fascinating ways. They have a million neurons in a cubic millimeter brain. They have one of the most complex communication systems in the animal kingdom. It has been documented that when a bee returns from searching for food sources, it will do a "dance" that, depending on the angle the bee assumes, the figure it "draws," and the speed at which the bee shakes, can indicate to other bees from the hive where the food source is. The beautiful thing about bees is the role they play for the whole of their community. Each of them dedicates their lives to serving the greater good. From worker bees to foragers, cleaner bees, drones, undertakers, guards, temperature controllers, builders, and nurses (that are said to check on larvae, on average, more than a thousand times per day), every bee does its part for the survival of its colony.

CONSIDER

Consider how all the bees take on different roles to help the hive operate not only effectively and efficiently, but so that it increases in longevity. Consider your roles in your life—those you take on in your family, at work, with your friends, and in your other relationships. Consider who those roles benefit. We take on roles that are beneficial to ourselves. We take on roles that are beneficial to others. But let's remember the bees and seek to be committed to those roles that serve the "colony" as a whole. Often, say in a relationship with a partner, we are expected to do jobs and tasks that serve the other. Other times, we only engage in those jobs that serve ourselves. But imagine if whatever role you took on was helping to maintain, sustain, and even improve not only you as an individual, or your partner as an individual, but the relationship itself?

CONNECT

Reflect on the roles you play in your life. Make a list of them. Write up a "job description" next to each one. (For instance, as a child of your parents, what roles do you have that fall under both a spoken and unspoken agreement?) Do all of your roles serve the highest good for the other, yourself, and the whole of the relationship? If not, consider adjusting, which may mean communicating that anticipated change to others, and adopt the intention to serve only in roles that are both healthy and beneficial for everyone. Make a step-by-step plan on how to adjust your roles. Reflect daily on your progress.

*I play an important and vital role—
in my commitments to my planet,
my community, my career, and
in my family and friend groups. I
commit to dedicating myself to the
roles that are healthy and serve the
greatest good of all, and to identify
and gently let go of those that don't.*

A Bird and Gentleness

The yellow-rumped warbler is a beautiful little feathered bird that lives in the Midwest of the United States. The female makes a small nest out of twigs and pine needles and other building supplies that the male brings her. She lines the nest with softness—with deer hair and lichen. Maybe moss. But what's most interesting is that she weaves this nest in such a way that the softness curls up and then covers the fragile eggs.

CONSIDER

What if we surround ourselves with softness? We can allow warblers to inspire us to not only create a "nest" by surrounding ourselves with people who gently support us, but also where the gentleness, nonviolence, and peacefulness that reaches up and surrounds us comes from within. Imagine that your self-talk is no longer harsh or negative. You don't shower shame on yourself or give in to guilt. You take extra care to weave softness toward others too, recognizing in one another the times we are extra fragile and deserve warmth instead of judgment. You forgive yourself and others. And you realize that mistakes can often crack hard shells, leaving yourself softer in the way you experience the world. You accept that mistakes are a valuable part of the human experience—and learning and growing and loving, gently and softly, are too.

CONNECT

▶ Sit in silence, perhaps in nature, and explore the ways you might be harsh, judgmental, and unforgiving of yourself. (Avoid taking on additional negative emotions about this realization; simply develop an awareness.) Envision how you could change that self-talk and self-reflection to one of honoring the whole of you. Talk to yourself with gentleness the way you would to a child or a loved one; the way you would to something or someone that is sacred. Consciously commit to doing at least one act of gentleness for yourself each day.

- Now, extend this gesture to others. Think about the people in your life. Is there someone who would benefit from extra "softness"? Create an intention (and a plan) to deliver softness to this person, whether it is with a gentle word, kind deed, prayer, or positive thought. Explore your feelings around this nonviolent, peaceful approach.

- For the next week, as you wake each morning, set a goal to offer "softness" in some way to someone else and to yourself. Reflect on your experiences at the end of each day.

Amid my strength is a softness, a nonviolent peacefulness that I honor and nurture. I allow it to cushion my relationships. I use it as the way I deliver love, empathy,

understanding,
forgiveness, kindness,
and honor. I use
it in all the ways I
communicate and
spend time with
others, myself, and
our living planet.

Butterflies and Perspective

When hiking through a rainforest, you might come across a special splash of blue—butterfly wings. Beautiful to the eye, but there is less there than meets the eye. That's because the blue morpho butterfly isn't truly blue, but instead, has wing scales that are shaped in ridges that bend in the sunlight and allow us to perceive a blue light wave. That makes us interpret and believe that the butterfly's wings are blue. And what's more, butterflies can see things we can't—things that are there. They can see ultraviolet waves, which helps them distinguish between flowers to find a source of sustenance.

CONSIDER

Let blue butterflies be a reminder that things aren't always as they seem at first glance. The story we tell ourselves about a situation, a person, a relationship, is how we interpret and believe it, but isn't necessarily reality. In addition, others may see things differently than us, and not only is it important to give them space to do that, but it is also important to understand that those different perspectives, if we take the opportunity to consider them, can help us see things that we were unable to before. A wider perspective can help you be more understanding, more compassionate, and kinder. It can help alleviate struggles in your relationships, avoid conflict, and nurture growth. Imagine giving one another the freedom to *be* by discovering how others perceive the world, instead of assuming you know or expecting that others perceive the world the way you do. By allowing differences without discrimination or judgment, you can embrace others' uniqueness and learn from their perspectives. Seeing things from a different, broader perspective helps us understand and experience truth.

CONNECT

▶ The next time you begin telling yourself a story about a situation or another person without really knowing if it is true, *pause*.

▶ Take a moment to think about the butterfly and remember how what meets the eye may not be the truth. Then, focus on your emotions. How does the story you're telling yourself make you feel? Are these emotions tempting you to react in a way that has more to do with the story you are telling yourself than what you *know* to be true?

▶ Next, as you become aware of how your emotions may have been hijacked by the story you were telling yourself, instead of giving airtime to these emotional thoughts, step back and remind yourself about the blue butterfly and the fact that you may not have the capacity to access how things really are for the moment.

▶ Finally, take this opportunity to let go and allow things to simply *be*, however they are, whether you are able to see it clearly or not. With this space, free from the turbidity caused by stories we tell ourselves, you won't expend extra energy on assumptions and false perceptions. Instead, you will create the opportunity for truth to reveal itself while enjoying peace and tranquility instead of struggle and suffering.

I trust in the universe to be as it is. Instead of creating a story based on my limited vantage point, I remind myself to pause and allow space for truth to reveal itself. I respond instead of react. I seek to witness from a wider perspective, and I find joy in being mindful in each moment—allowing truth to reveal itself.

Chameleons and Growth

Chameleons have a number of fascinating traits. They can change color, in part, to express their mood and to help maintain optimal body temperature. They can pivot their eyes separately to see from different angles at the same time. But what is extra interesting about these reptiles is that chameleons never stop growing. And while they grow so slowly that the growth is barely noticeable, for the duration of their lifetime, they will continue to expand.

CONSIDER

Remembering the chameleon as we move through stages of our lives can inspire us to adopt a lifestyle of perpetual growth. It is easy to get caught up in our daily routines and the "rinse-repeat" patterns of life. So it can benefit us to make an effort to seek and create opportunities to expand. Striving to make room to grow and improve gives you humility and grace. It can open you up for experiences that can greatly enrich your relationships with yourself and with others during our time on this planet.

CONNECT

Make it a goal to seek out and find at least one opportunity a day to grow. This could be something that doesn't take much time or effort, such as learning the definition of a new word, trying a new recipe, or even reading a new entry in this book. Record this new growth at the end of each day. Then, add a monthly goal that will take a commitment of a bit more time and energy and will help you grow on a new level, such as dedicating more time to your spiritual life, dedicating yourself more devotedly to your meditation or yoga practice, reading religious or spiritual books, finding a spiritual guide, or spending more quality time in nature and your place of worship. Record how each of these pursuits enhances your life and reflect on these collective experiences at the end of each month by reading over the entries of your growth and expansion with gratitude.

I continually allow myself to be open to learning, growth, and expansion. I strive to stretch deeply in all ways into my true nature, challenging myself to be all that I am. This is a lifelong commitment.

Chicks and Synchronicity

Something amazing occurs between a chick and its mother in the moments before the egg cracks open. It is described as simultaneous pecking, and it happens from the inside out and the outside in. While the chick is inside the egg, pecking its way out, the mother is on the outside, gently pecking her way in to help her baby enter the world. If the mother is too aggressive, the baby may die. If the baby is too passive, the baby may die. It is the synchronistic action of the two that hatches the opportunity for the mother and chick to finally meet.

CONSIDER

Imagine the chick in the egg and the hen in the nest and allow it to inspire you to pay more attention to the synchronicities in our world. Gently welcome this unseen beauty to be seen. If we begin moving through life with less aggression as well as less passivity, and tune in to what is around us and what is within us, we could be privy to new births of experiences. And like a "peck" to crack the egg to reach our goal, we might realize and experience that the universe is working with us simultaneously toward the same goal.

CONNECT

Each morning when you wake up, and before getting out of bed, spend the first several moments envisioning whatever it is you are hoping for, for the day, as if it already is. Allow this awe and wonder to surge through your mind and spirit. Stave off reaching for your smartphone, checking your emails, even grabbing a cup of joe until you honor the possibilities of the day. Breathe in and out deeply through your nose, from your belly, and acknowledge that while you may have well-laid plans for the day, you trust the universe to have a part in it all, and you maintain a sense of awe and wonder and mystery as you begin the day. Continue to inhale and exhale this sentiment of a balance between what you hope to be and the mystery that will unfold. Close this morning session by placing your hands to your heart, bowing to whatever force you bow to, and giving gratitude for unknown blessings already on their way.

*I trust the forces of creation to work
in synchronicity with me, allowing
my life to be filled with abundance,
joy, and blessings that I desire
and imagine. I may not always
understand, but I do always trust.*

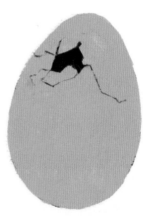

The Chrysalis and Struggle

On every continent except Antarctica, caterpillars change into butterflies. With more than seventeen thousand species of butterflies in the world, it seems that the blossoming of wings from caterpillar to chrysalis to flight is effortless. But what's interesting about the transition is that it takes a bit of a struggle for the butterfly to emerge. So while it may seem that the caterpillar easily pops from the chrysalis to be all that it can be, in fact, there's more to it, as there often is in the creation of a masterpiece. The butterfly's struggle to emerge is actually a necessary part of what helps the butterfly survive new butterfly-hood. Wiggling and moving to free itself forces a specific flying-power liquid into its never-before-used wings. If the chrysalis cracks open before the butterfly has struggled, the liquid would not flow as it should, and the butterfly's wings would not work. The struggle to emerge is what allows those beautiful wings to eventually unfold and fly.

CONSIDER

Take inspiration from the chrysalis when things change and get tough, and instead of wishing away the struggle, find gratitude in the strength it is building. Instead of *adding* to the discomfort of whatever is going on by fighting the struggle, recognize it, allow it, and settle into peace. You can lean into the unease and see it for what it is—an opportunity for a surge in power that will help you soar. Let go of identifying the struggle as only negative and instead see it as a growing opportunity. Shift your perspective and you may loosen the grip of fear around these difficult transitions and come to realize it can serve to help you stretch and soar.

CONNECT

Incorporate yoga with the chrysalis intention into your morning routine for the next week.

▶ Stretch deeply and mindfully, allowing each movement to surge new energy into the parts of your body that have been lying dormant overnight. While holding a pose, reflect on a recent past situation that was uncomfortable and challenging. Could you see now how that struggle helped make you stronger, or softer, or more compassionate?

▶ With each new pose, think about a current challenging situation that you are working through. Could you embrace a different perspective to see the struggle differently, respond to it differently, and appreciate the learning and growing that can come of it? Instead of focusing on how you can just get through the situation more quickly, and instead of looking for someone else to take on the burden, discover how you can take strength from it, how you can stay balanced through it, and how you can be more flexible while dealing with this difficult experience. Allow these feelings and sensations in your spirit to unify with your physical experience on the mat.

AFFIRMATION

I look at challenges as opportunities to grow, expand, strengthen, and become closer to my true and divine nature. As I physically stretch and strengthen my body, I feel my spirit stretch and strengthen too, unifying my mind, body, and breath.

Deciduous Trees and Expression

Trees such as aspen, maple, oak, and birch fill forests with lush greens for a summer season. But then, when days become cooler and nights shorter, the oranges, reds, and yellows of autumn leaves electrify the forest with brilliant colors. But this dazzling transition isn't because the leaves have changed into these new colors. Actually, what is most surprising is that deciduous tree leaves *are always* dazzling colors. They don't change INTO the colors that decorate autumn; simply put, the coming of fall, with its changes in temperature and sunlight, notifies trees to stop producing green. So the fall colors, always there in the leaves beneath the greens of summer, can now be revealed in their full splendor.

CONSIDER

What if we realize that life isn't about creating, forming, or forcing our true nature to be? Instead, it is simply about revealing it. Let the autumn trees inspire you to realize the vital importance of showing our own "true colors"—our inner human beauty in full splendor: kindness, empathy, warmth, consideration, strength. They are there not *in spite* of darker days, but *because* of them.

CONNECT

▶ Find a quiet, peaceful place. Sit in an upright position with your head, neck, and trunk aligned. Close your eyes. Bring your attention to your breath and breathe diaphragmatically, by inhaling through your nose and filling up your belly like a balloon and exhaling and allowing your belly to deflate toward your spine.

▶ Now allow yourself a moment to invite the struggle you are currently facing into your thoughts. Experience the physical and emotional sensations. Breathe into it and then take a deep exhale and let the breath go.

▶ Bring your thoughts to the trees and imagine the brilliant colors, ready to lighten and brighten darker days, under all the green. Then imagine these "colors" within you. What colors (passions, interests, feelings, characteristics) are within you, even if you don't see or display them right now, that could be revealed to brighten this situation? Is it love? Patience? Tolerance? Kindness? Strength? What colors of your true nature would be most beneficial to express at this time? Imagine these colors revealing themselves through intention and action.

▶ Allow these thoughts and emotions to fill yourself and breathe, inhaling and exhaling, for at least one minute with these sensations. Repeat this practice daily until you feel you've moved beyond the transition from struggle to strength through the expression of your true nature.

AFFIRMATION

I take comfort in the truth that I have a beauty and strength within me that can help during dark times. I find this beauty within and reveal it with love, humility, and fierce compassion.

Elephants and Nurturing

Mother-child bonds are everywhere on this planet and come in many forms. One of the most heartwarming is the elephant's. Their gestation period is the longest of any species—twenty-two months. Elephant moms stay with babies for about sixteen years. But one of the most endearing things about the mom-baby elephant relationship is the role other females play in the raising of these young pachyderms. At birth, a baby elephant is helped to stand by other females in their herd. The other females teach the calf how to nurse and eventually which plants to eat. And the moms and other female elephants and their children travel together in a circle, with the youngest members in the center to keep them safe. This caring for offspring not your own is called "allomothering," and is a critical factor in the successful raising of a calf in elephant herds.

CONSIDER

Consider the elephant when you have an opportunity to help support, protect, and guide someone younger or in need. While you may not take on the role of "mother" to another, being a mentor or teacher to someone else serves the greater good. Be someone who helps circle the younger or less wise. Share your talents, time, and resources in the circle of community.

CONNECT

Make it a goal to support or nurture someone in a positive way. This could be as simple as sharing supporting words or donating to nonprofits, or as complex as volunteering as a Big Brother or a Big Sister or becoming a foster parent to a child or even a pet. Think about ways you can be a positive supporter in your "circle."

I realize the beauty and importance of nurturing others. I consider myself a valuable member of the "circle" and take action to share my time and resources in a positive way.

Ferns and Learning

The spiral is a recurring shape that can be seen in patterns in nature. Tornadoes and hurricanes, seeds and seashells, are all on a planet that is a part of a spiraling galaxy. Among all the spirals, one of the most delicate and intricate is that of the fern—a vibrantly lush plant found throughout the globe. Unlike other plants, it doesn't have seeds or flowers, but instead reproduces with spores. It emerges and unfurls as a spiral, which protects the most delicate parts as it grows. Then it lives its life stretched and open. And when it is ready to die, some ferns do so the same way they began, in the intricate shape of a spiral.

CONSIDER

Allow the fern to remind us of the spiral of life. In our journey, it may seem that we pass the same point over and over. For instance, we might find ourselves in relationships that have the same issues, or jobs that have the same challenges. But the fern can remind us that each experience, if we are open to learning and growing, is instead an advancement on the "spiral," which gives us the opportunity to witness similar experiences from different perspectives. As we move toward wisdom and fulfillment and to coming into full being, if we embrace life as a nonlinear path that spirals toward enlightenment, we can have gratitude for the opportunities to grow little by little while simultaneously progressing in a beautiful life.

CONNECT

As a part of your movement practice, take a few moments each day to spin.

▶ Stand in an upright position in a safe space. Spin slowly and gently in clockwise circles. Begin with only a few repetitions.

▶ To avoid feeling dizzy, focus your attention on a visual point, or Drishti, and keep that point in focus as you begin to spin. When you need to take your eyes off the point to complete the spin, allow your head to turn and then land back on that focus point.

▶ Increase the number of rotations every day until you spin a total of twenty-one times. This practice can be enjoyed as a potent form of sensory input that, in part, enhances the vestibular system, and helps develop balance and depth perception.

▶ As you begin to develop stronger balance physically, you'll find balance and clarity on other levels as well, which will aid you as you continue on the spiraling learning journey.

AFFIRMATION

I feel gratitude on the path of wisdom that is built from the layering of experiences. I appreciate the opportunity to revisit situations and experiences with new vantage points as a way to learn and grow, in spiral progression, like the fern gently unfolding into life.

Fireflies and Finding Your Own Rhythm

Many firefly species hang out in grasses during the day and launch into the inky air at night. They have a remarkable liquid in them that lights them up. Even as larvae, many can light up and be seen under thin layers of dirt as tiny lights. But what is most interesting about these insects is that each firefly species blinks in its own rhythm, disappearing into the darkness one moment and lighting up their corner of the sky in the next. Each species blinks and twinkles in a particular pattern, uniquely its own.

CONSIDER

Be inspired by the firefly who lights up in its own rhythm. When you have the option to do what you feel is intrinsically right for you instead of following the crowd, follow your own truth. This might mean choosing to be alone instead of with those who you may not resonate with, or who have an energy that is less than positive or is even toxic. It might mean walking away from a job that you know doesn't fulfill your purpose or ending a relationship that doesn't nurture your true nature. Whatever it is, allow the firefly to remind you to find and use the strength to gently walk from that which doesn't help you live your light toward that which supports your beautiful brilliance.

CONNECT

Learn and use Bhastrika, or the bellows breathing technique.

▶ Sitting in an upright position, begin to breathe diaphragmatically, allowing the belly to expand on the inhale and move toward the spine on the exhale.

▶ When you are competent in this breathing technique, and you are able to belly breathe without needing to concentrate on doing it, then begin to forcefully exhale and inhale through both nostrils at the same time: a short, intense inhalation and then a short, intense exhalation.

▶ Repeat the inhale and exhale, without a pause in between. Do this for three rounds made up of seven to ten breaths per round. Breathe in a relaxed way in between rounds.

This Bhastrika technique is calming and relaxing, and the rhythmic breathing can help balance you, giving you a clearer mind to move forward in your own nature. Choose this practice on days when you are seeking clarity. (Check with your doctor before practicing.) This practice is best done in the morning to help set the tone for your day.

AFFIRMATION

I have a bright light that I shine and share in my own way with my own timing. I unapologetically give myself permission to fully honor myself through the expression of my beauty and truth with my unique rhythm.

Flies and Love

Flies can see in all directions without moving their eyes. While humans can process around 60 images a second, a fly's processing capacity hones in on around 250 images a second. But what might be most remarkable, perhaps, isn't a fly's sight, but its sound. While to most, the incessant buzzing of the housefly is irritating, the buzz is actually hummed in the key of F. The key of F is the same key as the heart chakra vibration in humans. Chakras are thought to be concentrated energy centers, or spinning disks of energy, in the human body, and each is related to a key. So our heart center has a resonant frequency of F. That means that the average houseflies are unintentionally singing, for all practical purposes, a love song.

CONSIDER

A fly can remind us that everyone sings their love song in their own way. There's always room to work in a relationship, and that can mean being more open to the way our romantic partner, friend, or family member expresses their love while simultaneously being witness to how graciously we receive it. If we are irritated and "bugged" in the way someone expresses their love because it doesn't match our expectations, we can work to better the relationship by adjusting how we react to that "love song." While it is our responsibility to decide if a relationship is one worth staying in (and it is always prudent to leave one that is unhealthy), it's also important to remember that it isn't our place to judge another's way of expressing their tune of love. Instead, see that person through your own eyes of love and appreciation while letting go of judgment. And be in tune with your way of receiving, because gracious receiving is an important way to love another as well.

CONNECT

▶ Before drifting to sleep at the end of the day, close your eyes for a moment and think about someone you care about but who "bugs" you in the way they show (or seemingly don't show) their love for you.

▶ Now shift your attention to your breath. Breathe deeply, in and out, slowly and mindfully, allowing sensations of everyone you love to enter your consciousness. Breathe the intention of love out to the world and imagine it reaching far beyond your aura.

Breathe the love of the universe into your full being. Allow the person who "gets under your skin" into this aura of love, letting go, at least for the moment, of the irritating characteristics of the person.

▶ Allow yourself to maintain that gentle feeling of love while discovering a different perspective about the person and the way they demonstrate their affection. Shower them with understanding and empathy.

▶ Continue to breathe this vibration of love, blanketing everyone, those you love easily and those you are challenged to love, with this vibration from your heart. Breathe this in and out until you drift off to sleep.

I vibrate in the key of love. I maintain this high vibration, allowing it to inspire everything I do, the

*ways I think, and
the perspectives I
see. I appreciate and
honor that others
express their love in
their own ways.*

Geese and Unity

Geese may be most widely known for the V-shaped formation they fly in as they migrate at the end of the season. As these larger-feathered birds fly, their wings create a draft or a lift of air. The V formation allows the flying range to be greater for the birds than if each one flew alone. It is so beneficial that if one of the birds falls out of formation, it feels the "drag" and rejoins the flock to take advantage of that uplift. And when the lead goose gets too tired to continue to guide the others, it drops back and another goose takes the lead. But probably the most heartwarming act of migrating geese is that when one of their flock gets hurt or wounded and drops out of the formation, two others drop out as well, to stay with the injured goose until it recovers.

CONSIDER

Geese have a lot to teach us about what it means to be loyal to a team and the individuals who are part of the team. What if we contemplate and act on the notion that everyone is important in our "flock" and that we should support each other more and compete against each other less? This includes our partners and spouses, immediate and extended family, friends, coworkers, and community. These individuals are all a part of our flocks. But we can also extend this "flock commitment" to all living beings—to those people we haven't even met. And to wildlife and our living planet. When you take on a commitment to and of unity and drop divisive tendencies, you can feel more peaceful and more cooperative. You will be inspired to act out of generosity instead of selfishness, and you will feel a different level of love and acceptance. You will be less judgmental and more kind. When you surround yourself with those who are loyal, your own loyalty to others and to your true nature will be more appreciated. When you cherish the bonds you make and the inclusion you feel with those around you and the planet in its entirety, you'll feel gratitude and nurturance. And this deep feeling of unity, of being a part of the global, universal consciousness flock, eliminates loneliness and supports you as you "fly."

CONNECT

Choose one person each week who may need your help, support, or simply your attention. Gently and unobtrusively take the time to think of them, write a note, send a text, make plans, drop off a surprise, or otherwise show your loyalty and love until they are ready to join back in the "flock." Consider doing this same act for a stranger (in a less personal way), perhaps by paying for someone's coffee behind you at the coffee shop, holding a door for someone, volunteering at a local food pantry, picking up any litter you find while on a hike in nature, or simply sitting at sunset and sending peaceful thoughts out into the world.

AFFIRMATION

I honor my relationships to those close to me and globally by devoting time, energy, and love to supporting others and our planet in meaningful ways that spread my loyalty and strengthen my commitment to peace and kindness.

The Hummingbird Nest and Expansion

There's a hummingbird that makes delicate nests to hold petite, jelly bean–size eggs snugly. But remarkably, amongst the velvety lining, woven twigs, bits of leaves, and plant fibers that keep the eggs cozy, warm, and safe is spider silk, which these petite birds use to thread their nests together and anchor them to wherever they've chosen to build their home. This silk isn't just to keep the building materials together. It serves an even greater purpose: It helps the nest expand. Cleverly integrated into the nest, these translucent filaments allow space for hatched babies to grow. The invisible threads stretch so the carefully woven fibers of the nest can expand, providing a space for fledglings to become all that they can be without being confined.

CONSIDER

We can learn to weave our own "silk web" into our "nests." Our
nests can be thought of as anything that holds us—anything that
we wrap around ourselves. They can be our structural homes, of
course, but also relationships, jobs, or daily routines—anything that
keeps us safe within perceived walls. If we accept and recognize
how these walls help us feel safe and keep dangers out, we can also
then recognize that without realizing it, these same walls might
hold us back from growing. If our space feels safe and comfortable,
we may inadvertently pass up on opportunities to expand into all
we can become. Consider taking a closer look at the "nests" you've
woven. Recognize your sources of safety and comfort, and then ask
yourself if you could go beyond them and challenge yourself to grow.
Are there relationships that are stagnant that you could explore
taking to deeper levels? Could you challenge yourself to reach for a
new position at work? Take on a new hobby? Or try something that
you've shied away from previously, like writing that book, painting
that picture, or going on that safari? By recognizing places in your
life that may be holding you back, and discovering ways you might
expand, you are weaving expandable webs into your nests so that
you can grow into your full potential.

CONNECT

▶ First, make a list of your "nests"—your home, your job, your relationships, your daily routines. Then, choose one item from the list and reflect on how it functions as a nest you are grateful for, writing down and giving gratitude for the ways and reasons it makes you feel safe, comfortable, and at ease.

▶ Now, consider if there are ways that the nest holds you back and keeps you from growing and expanding. How could you "weave in some expandable web"? Brainstorm specific ways you would go about moving beyond these safe boundaries you've set up.

▶ Then, in the upcoming days and weeks, begin to take action toward the expansion. When you feel accomplished in the expansion, revisit this exercise, explore the other "nests" on your list, and move toward more expansion.

I am flexible and create a life that allows me to expand continuously, gently moving beyond what previously held me back so I can become and express all that I already am.

Mole Rats and
New Ways of Listening

Mole rats, small creatures that live underground, have some pretty interesting traits. Some can move their upper teeth independently of each other. Some don't drink water, gaining all the moisture they need from the roots of plants. And some can go a very long time with little oxygen. But there is a truly fascinating species, the blind mole rat, that can communicate with seismic-patterned vibrations. They can send messages to one another by tapping their heads against the ceilings of their tunnels.

CONSIDER

What if we learned to be more aware of the subtle messages we otherwise might miss because we are tuned in to what is loudest? We usually pay attention to the loudest music, the loudest words, the "loudest" smells and tastes and sensations. What would we gain if we adopted new and subtler ways of listening? If we listened to others' words, actions, emotions, facial expressions, and body languages more? If we tuned in to the subtle messages our own bodies, minds, and spirits were sending to us? Let the tiny mole rat remind you that your powerfulness includes your sensitivity, and that it behooves you to quiet down enough to hear and really listen to one another and to yourself. Allow yourself to truly feel others, to truly hear what others are saying to you, versus what you want to hear or what you expect to hear. To truly listen to yourself. What if we were aware enough to receive messages that are coming from less obvious places, like the gentle vibrations of the earth?

CONNECT

Experience a mindful walk in nature. Move slowly and thoughtfully. Choose a place without others around where you can stop and close your eyes. If possible (and safe), take off your shoes so your feet can touch the earth. Now, become aware. Pause, and one by one, notice the sounds around you. Pause, and one by one, notice the smells. One by one, notice the sensations of the air on your skin, the feel of the earth under your feet. Notice how you are experiencing the fullness of the moment. Become aware of how, with intention, you are able to hear sounds you wouldn't normally notice, smell scents you would have missed, and feel sensations in your own body that you had previously tuned out. Practice this mindful walk in nature daily for the next week. Expand to engage in this mindfulness practice in any setting and at any time you can—when you are with people, when you are eating a meal, or when you are alone. Make mindfulness a lifelong daily practice.

AFFIRMATION

I make and take time each day for sacred stillness. In this divine time for myself, I allow all of my senses to recharge to keen awareness. I am becoming a better listener to nature, to others, to the world, and to myself.

Penguins and Relationships

In the coldest continent on the planet, emperor penguins exist in a world of ice, snow, and wintery skies. These waddling, flightless birds can dive hundreds of feet and hold their breath for twenty minutes. Their feathers form a barrier that is completely waterproof. But what is most remarkable is how the penguins behave in relationships—with their mate and with themselves. In most cases, they mate for life. In the male-female relationship, after the female lays one penguin egg, she carefully transfers it over to rest on top of the feet of her mate. She must do so quickly and delicately, so the egg isn't exposed to the bitter cold for too long. The male then carefully balances and holds the egg, on his feet, and presses his body down onto it to keep it warm. There's no nest to rest in—instead, he watches, protects, and incubates this egg in this upright position . . . for *two whole months*.

He doesn't eat during this watchful time but relies on the food stored up from his summer season of feasting. He is dedicated to his role in parenting, and so is the female partner. She is off traveling to the ocean to fill up on food after depleting her own supplies laying the egg. All the while he waits patiently with seemingly complete trust that his mate will come back when she is able. When the female returns home from her eating journey, they come together again.

CONSIDER

Consider focusing, like the penguins do, on staying true to your own role or obligations in a relationship instead of spending energy and thoughts doubting your partner. Whether it is a partnership in a marriage, in a friendship, in a working relationship, or with your child or sibling, the convergence is healthiest and strongest when each individual focuses on what they can give rather than what they can get. When you are fully vested in being the best for yourself and the one you are committed to, and your partner does the same, then you can trust in the relationship. Instead of expecting others to behave in the way we want them to behave, we can trust that they'll be in alignment with their own truths and truths that serve the greater partnership between you, if the partnership itself is for the highest good. Just like the female and male penguins each follow their own inner guidance system, which ends in returning to each other, if we trust each other to be our true selves—and be fully committed to the partnership—we will have a healthy foundation to build from. When we learn from and respect each other's natures, and truly appreciate each other for who we are regardless of what we can receive from the other, we foster trust—trust that we are equally committed to fulfilling the needs of the relationship. We can give and receive love unconditionally.

CONNECT

Reflect on a close relationship in your life (spouse, business partner, friend, child, sibling, etc.) and consider the penguin. Think about their dedication to their own roles in the relationship and use that to turn inward and reflect on your own roles in your relationship. If you stay aligned with your true nature, and express your nature consistently in the relationship, it is easier to allow your partner to do the same. This freedom to be your own true selves, and the resulting appreciation you exchange, turns the focus from expectations to gratitude, which is the building block for trust. In this same way, as the penguin allows its mate to go off for an extended amount of time, trusting that the mate will return, so too can you allow your partner in the relationship to be as they are meant to be, trusting in their commitment to their truth, which in part involves their dedication to you.

I remain consistently aligned with my true nature so others can trust me to be me. I seek relationships that honor my truth and surround myself with those who are consistently aligned with their own truth. I show gratitude for the relationships I have that are based on truth and trust and unconditional love.

Pine and Potential

There's a certain tree, the jack pine, that grows in vast boreal regions. Standing among its neighboring trees, this evergreen uses water and sunlight to grow and change, as most trees do. But unlike most trees, it has a special ability to survive the harshest conditions, such as a forest fire. Most remarkably, it not only can withstand a forest fire, but it actually *needs* a fire to propagate. Hidden within the canopy of these majestic beauties are millions of seeds held snug in cones. These seeds are cradled in the cones by resin that glues the cones shut. And it isn't until a wildfire spreads and the temperature in the forest significantly rises that the resin finally melts, and the seeds can be dispersed. The seeds then drift down to settle onto the cleared, burnt ground. When other trees haven't survived a fire, these seeds can be counted on to revive the forest and help it begin again.

CONSIDER

Life comes with its own "wildfires" that bring along destruction. But hidden in human nature are often seeds of potential that sometimes grow most brilliantly when tough times almost consume us. Let the jack pine inspire you to grow something new and beautiful from the destruction. When a wildfire comes into your life, see if you can see through the pain and allow seeds of inspiration to release new ideas (like starting a new business, volunteering, or making a change in your lifestyle) that can turn a tough time into something that helps you create more beauty in your life and in the world.

CONNECT

When you are struggling through a challenging situation, find some time during each day to be in nature. Sit on a fallen log, along a river, in a meadow, on a mountain, even in a park near a tree, and close your eyes.

- ▶ Listen to the sounds around you. Settle into the peace that surrounds you. Allow yourself to be cradled in this peace as you struggle with the pain.

- ▶ Then, with the peacefulness surrounding you, breathe into the pain for a moment—lean into it just a bit and define the specific feelings you are having that are wrapped into the pain itself (fear, abandonment, rejection, sadness, etc.). As you continue to breathe slowly and gently, explore an action that you could take that could begin to balance the pain with hope. For example, perhaps tied into the pain of losing a loved one is the fear that your memories about them will fade. Find balance away from that fear by considering an action to counter it, that can unlock potential, adding beauty to the world in the name of the loss.

▶ As you sit in nature listening to any feelings that arise that sound like new ideas, hope, or beauty, allow these thoughts to germinate, grow, and blossom.

▶ When you are ready, put them into action—action that improves, heals, rebuilds, or grows something beautiful out of the pain.

I allow the pain of what I'm going through to unlock potential and create inspiration—

inspiration that allows me to put my energy toward something that will serve the world for the highest good.

Redwoods and Altruism

If you've had the honor of standing next to a redwood tree, you've experienced the awe of seeing the sheer gigantic size of these ancient forest members. A giant redwood can reach up to 350 feet high with a diameter of over 20 feet. But what is even more inspiring than their size is their method of being. They are trees that give. Throughout their long lives, some more than a thousand years, they provide the earth with beauty, oxygen, shade, and peace. They connect underground in an intricate and expanding root system. And even when these trees die, as a final act of giving as they begin to decay, they send the nutrients they have absorbed over the years back into the earth, where they are received through the roots of other surviving trees in the forest. This community uses the nutrients to thrive and eventually replaces the dying tree with a new tree that will sprout up from its roots.

CONSIDER

Consider the redwood and reflect on the act of giving in a healthy way. Think of the powerful effect giving has on others, your community, and the world at large while at the same time benefiting you and your own life. Consider becoming a giver every day, like the redwood does just by being. Adopt the practice of giving in some way, each time you meet another person. Giving can be monetary— you could buy someone lunch, a meaningful gift, or donate to a global cause in the name of someone you know. But you can, of course, give in other ways too. You can offer a smile to a passerby, let someone cut in line while waiting in traffic, or spend time with someone by disconnecting from electronics and really listening, focusing, and being present. Think of the redwood tree when you have an option to either give or hold back and reserve. And make the choice to give.

CONNECT

Make a list of ways you can give in the next month. Include ways to give to people you know (friends, family, coworkers), to strangers, to the planet, and the world. See if you can come up with creative ways of giving in addition to volunteering time and spending money. Follow through with this list by choosing one thing from it each day. Take action. Remember, it doesn't have to cost anything—giving a laugh, a wildflower, a hug, or understanding contributes to the beauty of the world in small but profound ways. Reflect on your progress and the results daily. Doing this exercise repeatedly will inspire you to continue to give as a lifetime practice.

AFFIRMATION

I devote a portion of my resources—my heart, my time, my money, and my talent—to giving to others and the planet for the highest good, every day.

The Resurrection Plant
and Resilience

The resurrection plant is a primitive life-form, and in evolutionary terms, falls somewhere between mosses and ferns. It doesn't have true leaves but unfurls almost like a flower when given what it requires to thrive. What's most impressive about this ancient plant is that in the absence of sufficient nutrients and water, it can remain completely dormant and survive for up to eight full years. Once it is watered, the plant will revive, unfurling into all it was meant to be.

CONSIDER

We all have times that challenge us and make us thirst for what
we believe we need to survive. We might be lonely after breaking
up with someone or craving satisfaction in a job. We might feel
depleted in health or resources. But whatever it is, allow the
resurrection plant to remind you that you have profound resilience
to keep surviving. Use it to inspire you to stay consistent with a
practice that accesses your deep reserves, whether it is in the form
of physical movement (yoga, tai chi, working out, biking, going for a
run), spirituality (meditation, prayer, being in nature), or creativity
(baking, painting, writing, reading) . . . whatever it is that fills you
up with renewed energy and creative force. Spend time immersed
and mindful, knowing that your practice, whatever it may be, is
helping to strengthen and replenish you when you're going through
challenging times. It will help so that when things are back in
balance, you'll bloom again in your beautiful brilliance.

CONNECT

For the next week, commit to a daily yoga practice with the
intention of exploring resiliency. Focus on the poses that are
your least favorite, such as the ones you find most challenging
to do—the ones that tire you, make your muscles shiver and your
balance quiver. Sometimes the poses that are your least favorite and
challenge you the most are those that bore you or aren't necessarily
difficult physically, but they make you realize your inflexibility.
Choose to do these, each day, for a week.

- While holding each pose, explore the sensations you have, watching the transformation until the moment you feel you can't hold the pose any longer and want to get out of it. Become aware that this, the moment you want to get out, is the moment the pose begins. Settle into the experience of that moment.

- Close your eyes. Breathe. Let go of the thoughts that are trying to convince you to quit, and instead find that peaceful space between the inhale and exhale. Realize you have resilience, in this quiet space, to continue.

- As you do finally release from the pose, reflect on the confidence and poise you cultivated as you found strength and balance, even in discomfort. Come out of the pose with the same integrity as you went into it.

I am resilient, strong, and able to maintain even when conditions aren't optimal. I have faith that things will balance back to abundance in all ways

and I will have patience

until it does, all the

while resting in that

place within that is

powerful and strong.

Seahorses and Steadiness

Seahorses are fascinating fish. They are mostly monogamous. They can be found traveling through the ocean "holding tails" with their mate. They are excellent at camouflage. But what is most special about these spiny-tinys is their feeding habits. Instead of gobbling up meals when they come upon a food source, they take in sustenance almost constantly throughout the day, sucking in plankton through their trumpet-shaped snouts. Because they don't have teeth and don't have a stomach, they are required to eat virtually nonstop.

CONSIDER

Think about the seahorse when you move through the day by adopting a steadiness in your manner. This steadiness can be applied to all aspects of your self—mind, body, emotions, and breath. Instead of erupting with emotions or actions, learn to pause, consider, and respond instead of reacting. When something upsets or challenges you, remember to continue to breathe instead of holding your breath. Find that pause between the inhale and exhale. Steady the body in physical ways by engaging the muscles needed in a pose or activity while releasing those that aren't needed. Steady the mind through mantras and meditations. And be steady in your habits—not overdoing anything, not overeating, not overdrinking—doing nothing in excess. Steadiness can help eliminate anxiousness and that overwhelming feeling. It helps us feel more balanced—energetically, emotionally, mentally, and physically.

CONNECT

▶ Find a quiet place to sit in silence after dark and in a darkened space. Light a candle (a natural one without synthetic fragrances is optimal) and focus on the flame. Try not to blink. Breathe steadily, diaphragmatically, by allowing the belly to expand on the inhale and deflate on the exhale, breathing through the nostrils. Continue to gaze at the flame.

▶ After 30 seconds of gazing, gently close your eyes and repeat a mantra—a word or phrase that has meaning to you, that feels peaceful and calming. Repeat this mantra in your mind, over and over, syncing it with your breath. Keep a steady rhythm of this repetition. Do this practice for a few minutes until you begin to feel a steadiness in your demeanor, a calmness.

▶ When you feel ready, open your eyes, extinguish the candle, and reflect on your state of being. Repeat this practice nightly, until eventually you can translate this feeling of steadiness that you cultivate during your meditation into your life.

▶ When something threatens to disrupt your steady, peaceful demeanor, such as traffic, rushed meals, chaotic times at work, tense moments in relationships, even challenges in your yoga poses, draw back to the steady sensations from your meditation. Find a Drishti (like the flame—a point to focus on, literally or in your mind's eye), think about your mantra, remember the seahorse, and breathe in and out, steady and calm.

AFFIRMATION

I am steady through the currents of life. I do nothing in excess. I respond instead of react. I cultivate a steady mind, steady emotions, steady body, and steady energy. I keep my breath steady and even.

Seeds and Patience

The spring sun shines on the earth. The rain falls. Wildflower seeds sprout up and, inch by inch, reach into the sky, blossoming into their unique beauty. But while the warm rains and thawing earth contribute to the blooming spring life, what some seeds truly need to sprout isn't just a momentary rainfall or passing spots of sunshine. What they need is the long, drawn-out deep freeze of winter, waiting through the seemingly endless cold months so that in time they can grow. These seeds, called cold-stratified seeds, require a long time period, day after day, under the freezing earth to prepare to flower.

CONSIDER

Think about the cold-stratified seeds when you are waiting for things to change and wishing away the present moment. For those who live in wintery conditions, this might feel familiar if you find yourself losing patience while you wait for spring to come, wishing away the frigid months in between. But the need for patience isn't just for outside situations, but internal angst as well. Often, we become frustrated with any sort of waiting, such as waiting for a relationship to evolve, a job opportunity to present itself, or the inspiration to create something new. But instead of rushing and pressing, reflect on the seeds that need the long winter to germinate and realize that these times of waiting could in fact be giving you the exact conditions you need: opportunities to reflect, change, grow, heal, or be inspired. If you accept this time of dormancy with ongoing patience, moving through it with an appreciation and curiosity for what might be revealed, you'll be blessed with a peaceful ease through the process.

CONNECT

When you come into a situation that makes you wait—whether it is something minor like a long line in the grocery store, waiting for your phone to recharge, or being on hold with customer service, or something major, like waiting for test results, waiting for your house to sell, or receiving a promotion at work—think about the cold-stratified seeds and foster patience. Realizing that impatience fills the waiting time with stress, frustration, and angst, and that it serves no positive purpose, the next time you are faced with a wait (whether it is minor or major), witness it as an opportunity. Approach and embrace it with two questions:

▶ Can I be mindful and experience this moment as it is, instead of wishing for the future?

▶ How can I fill this precious waiting time I've been gifted with something positive—what can I accomplish that I wouldn't have been able to if I hadn't had this time?

Depending on how long the wait is, this could mean closing your eyes for a mindful moment of meditation as you are on hold, striking up a friendly conversation with the person in line who is waiting with you, filling the wait time for test results with a new exercise program, or writing a book you've always thought about writing as you wait for your house to sell. Approaching situations with patience gives you the opportunity to enjoy moments that otherwise would have been spent in angst and frustration. Seeing the wait as a way the universe or the powers you bow your head to is preparing you to be all that you can be can help you step back and be truly present in each moment you are blessed to experience. So each and every moment you are challenged to wait, see if you can transform the wait into an opportunity to experience more richness and peacefulness.

I am patient. I do not struggle with the wait. Instead, I embrace each moment as an opportunity to learn, transition, gain a new perspective, and enjoy my precious life.

Skunk Cabbage and Boundaries

The appropriately named skunk cabbage is a low-growing plant that emanates a skunk-like smell and can be found in wet woods, along creeks and in swamps. But what is most fascinating about this wild plant is that it has a remarkable ability to produce heat by breaking down sugar using oxygen. This plant-created heat melts ice and the snow around the plant in a perfect circle so the winter cold can't seep in and freeze or damage the plant, which allows the plant to emerge from the earth and bloom before winter is over. The heat that it emits makes it possible for the plant to grow upward when the ground is still frozen and while many other plants are still dormant in the ground.

CONSIDER

Think of the skunk cabbage and imagine an aura of warmth emanating from it. Now imagine yourself doing the same, allowing an aura of warmth to emanate from yourself. The skunk cabbage reminds us that we have the capacity to "melt" a circle around ourselves that exudes warmth, kindness, and love and that gives us the capacity to bloom in harsh moments when we might otherwise be "dormant." This aura around you is peaceful and loving, and it can protect you from others' negativity that may seep in and "freeze" or damage you. Others who come near you will feel this peaceful loving energy too. Be inspired by the skunk cabbage plant and break down barriers that are keeping you separate from others, expanding in your relationships to be who you are, in all of your blossoming glory.

CONNECT

▶ Close your eyes. Begin to breathe diaphragmatically. To do this, allow the belly to expand on the inhale like a balloon and deflate on the exhale. Breathing through your nose, slowly inhale and slowly exhale, without a pause between the inhale and exhale.

▶ Now, imagine yourself as a being that has an energy center of love. Imagine this love expanding through you and outside you, creating an aura of warmth, love, and grace that surrounds you and melts boundaries that previously kept you separate from others and from your true self.

▶ Do this exercise for 30 seconds, one time a day, preferably as the opening to your meditation session. Be aware of any positive changes in the way others respond to you, and how you feel about others, as a result of this lifelong practice.

AFFIRMATION

I am a warm and loving being. I am kindness. I am grace. This emanates from me and melts cold barriers around and within me to create a clear path for my love and light to grow, glow, blossom, and shine.

Snakes and Non-attachment

Gliding along the forest floor, a garter snake that usually appears darkish green has turned bluish. Its eyes are opaque and cloudy. And the snake seems to be moving more slowly than normal, somewhat sluggishly. But the snake is not sick. Instead, it is transitioning through the fantastic feat of shedding its outer skin. The snake has grown, and unlike many other animals on the planet, the snake's skin doesn't grow along with it. The skin has also accumulated parasites. So it is time for the snake to let this skin go. It finds a rock or another sharp edge, slices the skin—usually a small slit on the face—and begins to slowly, slowly emerge from the old skin. While it's shedding, its vision is clouded and it's more vulnerable. But days or even weeks later, the snake will completely release its old skin and slide away, letting go of what no longer serves it.

CONSIDER

Like the snake, we can detach from things that have previously been important to us. The skin that once served the snake and literally kept it together would in time harm it, so it simply lets the skin go. We can do the same. Without clinging to relationships, objects, jobs, and places, we can appreciate and have gratitude for them, and then when we outgrow those things, we can let go. Explore whether something has been parasitic and is no longer serving you. Have you "grown too big for your old skin"? Have you expanded in your thoughts and feelings, becoming different enough that you realize you need to glide away from old habits, relationships, or situations and start anew? Let the snake inspire you to realize what no longer serves you. Slow down so that you move through the transition mindfully and peacefully. You can accept, without struggle, how things during the transition might seem cloudy and unclear. Understand that you might feel more vulnerable, but continue moving away from the old "skin." Trust and appreciate the process.

CONNECT

Identify something that you own or a habit that you have—something that you know, intuitively, doesn't serve you in the way it once did. Make the commitment to let it go.

▶ Do it slowly, thoughtfully, mindfully, gently, kindly. But do it, so that you can grow fully into who you are now.

▶ Then reflect on the process of letting go. How did it feel? Was it scary? Did you feel resistant? Did it make you feel vulnerable? Explore the process.

▶ And then, explore the outcome. How has your life changed? How has the letting go enhanced your situation, relationship, or life? Embrace the experience in its entirety and give gratitude for your wisdom to move forward, expand, and release.

I willingly let go of layers of myself that no longer serve me. I gently walk away from unhealthy relationships, jobs, commitments, and objects that no longer serve me and the highest good. I move slowly through transitions so that I emerge clearly and resolutely into more of my true nature.

Spider Silk and Faith

Spiders' silk has long been known as a remarkable substance that can't quite be replicated by humans. This air-colored filament is used in a variety of ways by arachnids and woven into everything from intricate flat webs to bucket-shaped funnels. Spiders' silk can help them soar through the sky in silky balloons. They can also use their silk to communicate with one another or mark their territories, and some even wrap their eggs in silk to protect their unborn babies. But what's most spectacular is that some spiders create draglines. What looks like one strand of web is often many strands stuck together. It hardens as soon as the liquidly silk hits the air. This strong web is like an invisible rope to guide the spider back home if they fall or drop.

CONSIDER

What if, like a spider that tosses its silk into the breeze without knowing where it will land, we move forward in life with the freedom to explore and take chances, all the while holding on to the comfort in knowing we have a dragline—a "lifeline" that will bring us back home? Trying something new, like a different job, opening a business, or moving to a different home in an unknown city—these all can bring great rewards, but the unknowns can seem scary. Weaving a dragline made of faith can reassure you that you have something to lean on, turn to, and believe in during the challenging times of your new venture. This guideline can be rooted in your deeply held beliefs, your religion, or your spirituality. When you feel lost or insecure in a new situation, let the spider inspire you to find your way back to your source, whatever you believe that to be. Know that this lifeline is stronger than anything, seen or unseen. Look to the spider's silk to inspire you to fill your life with such faithful devotion to your source of truth.

CONNECT

▶ Close your eyes. Release all the tension in your forehead, eyelids, and eyebrows. Bring your attention to your third eye, the space between your eyebrows near where the pineal gland resides. Allow the eyes to gently gaze in this direction, to the third eye, with your eyelids still closed. Breathe in and out through your nose deeply and diaphragmatically, allowing the belly to expand on the inhale and deflate on the exhale. Keep your attention on the third eye.

▶ Now, begin to pray or otherwise communicate in whatever way you do to whoever you bow your head to, giving thanks for unknown blessings already on their way. Feel this belief and trust surge through you like the powerful force that it is. Allow it to give you confidence to continue to move forward into the unknown.

▶ As you connect to your third eye and then move into prayer, listen for subtle messages that help open the communication of intuition. Feel this "dragline" and breathe in and out confidence in this connection. Incorporate this into your daily meditation as a part of your lifelong practice.

AFFIRMATION

Each time I throw out my dragline, I act with complete faith that I am connected to my deepest inner self and source, giving me confidence and the freedom to explore and experience fully without fear. I know I can always come back by following my guideline, which is my faith.

Trees and Balancing Strength with Flexibility

The plants that we walk among and call trees are remarkable. These skyward growers have a variety of fascinating traits. There are those that have rings in their trunks that can indicate times of drought and flooding. There are those that contain bundles in their trunks that are like straws wrapped in a ring of cells, helping conduct the flow of water. But it is the parts working together—the roots sinking into the earth and the branches and leaves stretching high into the sky—that make these oxygen growers scattered across our earth impressive. Their root systems offer strength and stability, while their branches and leaves provide flexibility. Both strength and flexibility help them survive and thrive in even the harshest conditions.

CONSIDER

Allow trees to remind us of the value and importance of being both strong and flexible in a situation. Strength allows you to stay true to who you are, so you aren't blown off course, while flexibility allows you to see others' perspectives without judgment, and to be able to adjust, learn, grown, change, and expand. Both are skills that need to be practiced and nurtured, and it is important to be aware of skill-building both. Too much strength and you become rigid in your thinking and being, shutting out opportunities to grow and expand in situations and relationships. Too much flexibility means little to no boundaries, and you may move into situations or relationships that aren't aligned with your beliefs and your truths. Therefore, it is important to continually rebalance these two skills.

CONNECT

Choose a yoga pose or series of poses to practice with the intention of strength and flexibility for the next week. Each time you take to the mat, become aware of each pose and feel both your strength and flexibility in the pose. When you get off the mat, take this with you into the world—this ability to apply strength and flexibility in not only the physical world, but the emotional and spiritual world as well. Remember the tree and visualize how you could express these characteristics in a particular situation. Imagine the outcome if you balanced both your strength and flexibility. This can be applied to all aspects of your life, such as relationship dilemmas, conflicts with work, or even struggles with yourself over challenging decisions. Feel gratitude for your ability to stay balanced.

AFFIRMATION

I am both powerfully strong in my commitment to my nature, and fluidly flexible in my ability to grow, change, adapt, and understand other perspectives. I am grateful for my balanced approach and way of being.

The Wild and
Your Life's Work

Every part of nature has a purpose, and each and
every thing acts and lives its purpose completely
and wholly. Each seed, chick, kit, and pup expresses
only its truth, in the way it grows and eats and
survives and communicates. We learn much from
nature, but one of the primary lessons is that nature
is always true to itself. Our true nature, if we are
open to experiencing it, is to follow the wisdom of
the wild—both to be fully ourselves and to share the
beauty of our essence with the world, which in turn
contributes to the betterment of all.

CONSIDER

Be inspired by every element of life in nature. Anytime you doubt your place, your role, or your path, think about something in nature. Know that like each tree, skunk, snail, and songbird, you have a unique and important role to play that balances and helps create purpose and beauty in the world.

Remember how each being and plant unequivocally stays true to its own nature. Allow this to inspire you to truly know your own nature, to explore your own gifts and passions, and to live, without hesitation or apology, your remarkable, beautiful truth. Be *you*. Live your light!

CONNECT

Find a favorite place in nature. While there, connect with the wild by being mindful and aware. Settle into your own spiritual practice, through meditation, prayer, or whatever is meaningful to you.

▶ When you've come to a place of stillness, begin to contemplate the ways you can be and express who you uniquely are in your full splendor. In your relationships, in your job. In your home: how you decorate and fill your space with meaningful objects. In your life: who you keep company with. In your hobbies and activities: through art—painting, writing, dancing, singing, composing music, sculpting. Think about a mission statement or a description or a mantra of YOU. Learn it. Repeat it. Live it.

▶ Then, find ways, every day, to express this mission, mantra, your inner and most beautiful and true nature. Make a list of these ways and accomplish at least one form of expression each day, until in time, it is a regular practice to express your true nature in everything you do and say and all the ways you are. Remember to embrace, applaud, and honor who you are, always. Like other activities in this book, this is an ongoing practice that you can return to regularly throughout your life.

AFFIRMATION

I honor the divinity within myself. I discover and embrace my true nature and I allow my life work to be, being myself. *I love myself and know that I am a creative, powerful force of nature who helps balance, beautify, and make better the planet I live on. Every day,* I live my light.

Acknowledgments

I'd like to thank my talented and insightful editor, Deanne, and the fantastic team at Chronicle Books. Thank you for believing in this project and for helping it to become as it is.

Thank you to those who helped me discover my place with nature, way back when I was a little girl—my parents and grandparents and brothers. Thank you to my teachers and my students along the way—all of whom I've learned much from. Thank you to my three daughters, who joined me, when they were welcomed into the world, with a love for all things wild. Thank you to those that walk the trail with me—those that have all along, and those that were there as I wrote this book: my family and extended family, my friends, colleagues, and guides. Finally, thank you to the power that I bow my head to, for gifting us the natural world from which to grow, learn, and be. Nature—around and within—is a beautiful place to call home.

 142

About the Author

Jennifer Ziegler, Hope Lake Photography

Sheri Mabry was born in a small town in Wisconsin. She spent much of her childhood in the woods, along creeks and near lakes, seeking and discovering the treasures of the wild. Now Sheri blends her appreciation of nature with her foundation of yoga and meditation, her passion to write, and her inspiration to create. She writes books for children and adults, creates art, and offers writing and yogic services. She is blessed with wonderful family and friends and is always grateful for time together in the mountains and on the trail. To learn more about Sheri, visit www.sherimabryinc.com.